DESSERTS

DESSERTS

PERFECTLY PREPARED TO ENJOY EVERY DAY

This edition published in 2012
LOVE FOOD is an imprint of Parragon Books Ltd

Parragon
Queen Street House
4 Queen Street
Bath BA1 1HE, UK

www.parragon.com

ISBN: 978-1-4454-6752-8

Printed in China

Concept: Patrik Jaros & Günter Beer
Recipes and food styling: Patrik Jaros www.foodlook.com
Text: Günter Beer, Gerhard von Richthofen, Patrik Jaros, Jörg Zipprick
Photography: Günter Beer www.beerfoto.com
Photographer's assistants: Sigurd Buchberger, Aranxa Alvarez
Cook's assistants: Magnus Thelen, Johannes von Bemberg
Designed by Estudio Merino www.estudiomerino.com
Produced by Buenavista Studio s.l.www.buenavistastudio.com
The visual index is a registered design of Buenavista Studio s.l. (European Trademark Office number 000252796-001)
Project managment: trans texas publishing, Cologne
Typesetting: Nazire Ergün, Cologne

Notes for the Reader
This book uses both metric and imperial measurements. Follow the same units of measurement throughout; do not mix metric and imperial. All spoon measurements are level: teaspoons are assumed to be 5 ml, and tablespoons are assumed to be 15 ml. Unless otherwise stated, milk is assumed to be full fat, eggs and individual vegetables are medium, and pepper is freshly ground black pepper.

The times given are an approximate guide only. Preparation times differ according to the techniques used by different people and the cooking times may also vary from those given. Optional ingredients, variations or serving suggestions have not been included in the calculations.

Recipes using raw or very lightly cooked eggs should be avoided by infants, the elderly, pregnant women, convalescents and anyone suffering from an illness. Pregnant and breastfeeding women are advised to avoid eating peanuts and peanut products. Sufferers from nut allergies should be aware that some of the ready-made ingredients used in the recipes in this book may contain nuts. Always check the packaging before use.

The publisher would advise using fish and seafood from sustainable sources.

Picture acknowledgements
All photos by Günter Beer, Barcelona

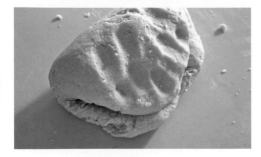

Contents

Introduction

Desserts are the culinary climax of a successful meal, the final course that leaves your family and guests feeling pleasantly replete.

The world of desserts is very diverse. From light fruit-based sweets and creamy puddings to oven-baked specialties, there is something to suit every taste. The dessert is the last course of a menu and should be chosen with care – after all, it makes the final impression and is the one guests take home with them. It's also important that the dessert complements the rest of the menu. If you remember just a few small points, you can't really go wrong. For example, after heavier courses, it's advisable to go for lighter, fruity desserts so that your guests are not left feeling too full. If the first courses are less filling, you can serve a more substantial dessert. In the summer, cool fruit and ice cream desserts offer welcome refreshment, while in the autumn or winter months, richer, warming puddings go down a treat.

If you choose a certain national cuisine to be the theme of your menu, make sure the dessert complements this. For example, it's best to serve a French dessert with a French menu, Wine Chaudeau or Baked Peaches with Lavender, perhaps. An Italian meal can be rounded off with Zabaglione or Panna Cotta. For an Asian meal, on the other hand, Tapioca-coconut Pudding, Spring Rolls with Cherry Filling or Fried Fine Noodles in Strawberry Gazpacho would make an excellent choice.

Fruit

Fruit-based desserts go with virtually any menu and can be varied in a multitude of ways. They can be refined with exotic fruits, dried fruit, fine sweet sauces (you can find a selection of these on pages 12–13), nuts or liqueurs, and adapted to all kinds of menus. When using fruit, especially berries, do make sure you buy seasonal, local produce whenever possible. These have more flavour than imported goods. Frozen berries that have been harvested in the appropriate season are also a far better choice than imported produce.

Remember, what applies to every other course also applies to desserts: the higher the quality of the ingredients, the better the finished dish!

Chocolate

Chocolate desserts are not only favourites with children, they're also a popular choice with adults. To guarantee the perfect chocolate treat, always use superior-quality chocolate. If a recipe specifies plain chocolate, such as Plain Chocolate Mousse, use chocolate with a 70% cocoa content. This is more expensive than chocolate with a lower cocoa content, but it's far more intense and gives the dessert a very distinct flavour. Strictly speaking, white chocolate is not really chocolate since it contains cocoa butter rather than cocoa. If using white chocolate, for example for White Chocolate Mousse with Maple Syrup, buy a product with a high cocoa butter content.

For recipes containing cocoa powder, such as Tiramisù, use an unsweetened, low-fat product. Cocoa should never be substituted with a chocolate drink powder because this does not contain the required amount of cocoa and is far too sweet.

Decoration

In no other course is decoration as important as in the dessert. This is where you can give your creativity full reign. Fruit, especially berries, makes attractive garnishes, while candied petals, such as violets, roses or pansies, can turn a simple dessert into a work of art. But some desserts look good without additional embellishment. In such cases, simply dust with a little icing sugar or cocoa powder, or add a few sprigs of fresh herbs, such as lavender, mint or lemon balm. Other decorations not only look good but will give your dessert additional flavour. This is true of roasted, chopped nuts, chocolate curls and shavings and the grated zest of citrus fruits. Sweet sauces and syrups can also add a splash of colour to desserts and enhance flavours. Bavarian Cream, for example, is usually served with a fruity sauce. Some desserts, such as ice creams, are often served with one or two home-baked biscuits or brownies.

Equipment
You don't necessarily need to buy expensive kitchen gadgets to prepare different desserts, but there are some utensils that will certainly make preparation a lot easier. A good set of kitchen scales is a worthwhile investment because the quantities stated in recipes need to be observed exactly when making desserts. A good hand whisk is also useful. You will need a balloon whisk to prepare light cream desserts and sauces made over a bain marie. Good non-stick

baking tins prevent oven-baked desserts sticking or collapsing when inverted. To make the delicious, low-fat White Chocolate Mousse with Maple Syrup, you will need a siphon.

A piping bag with interchangeable nozzles will allow you to pipe attractive decorations onto gateaux, cream desserts and ice cream. A chef's blowtorch gives a professional finish to a whole range of desserts that would otherwise have to be browned under the grill.

How to use this book

Unless otherwise stated, the recipes in this book are intended to serve four.

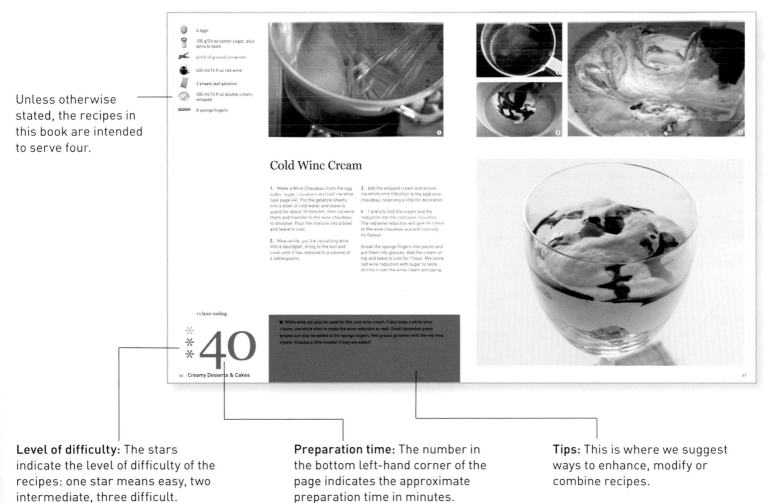

Level of difficulty: The stars indicate the level of difficulty of the recipes: one star means easy, two intermediate, three difficult.

Preparation time: The number in the bottom left-hand corner of the page indicates the approximate preparation time in minutes.

Tips: This is where we suggest ways to enhance, modify or combine recipes.

 8 eggs

125 g/4¼ oz sugar

pinch of salt

60 g/2¼ oz plain flour

40 g/1½ oz cornflour

Sponge Cake

1. Preheat the oven to 190°C /375°F/ Gas Mark 5. Separate the eggs and put the egg yolks into a mixing bowl. Reserve four of the egg whites. Store the remaining egg whites in the refrigerator for later use. Add 60 g/2¼ oz of the sugar to the egg yolks.

2. Beat together the egg yolks and sugar for about 5 minutes, until the mixture is pale yellow.

3. Slowly beat the four egg whites with the salt in a separate bowl. Stir in the remaining sugar a little at a time. Beat with an electric mixer on medium speed, until holding stiff peaks, then beat on the highest speed for a further 30 seconds. Add the beaten egg whites to the egg yolks and carefully fold them in with a rubber spatula.

4. Sift together the flour and cornflour into the mixing bowl.

5. Carefully mix them in using a rubber spatula, without hitting the sides of the bowl. This would 'shock' the cake batter and prevent it rising properly.

6. Line a 30 × 40-cm (12 × 16-inch) baking tray with baking paper, pour in the mixture and smooth it. Bake in the preheated oven for about 10 minutes until golden. Remove from the oven and leave to cool slightly before using.

■ To make a chocolate sponge cake, fold in 20 g/¾ oz of low-fat cocoa powder, then bake as directed. Chocolate sponge cake tastes really delicious as a Swiss roll filled with cherries and cherry jam.

✳
✳ 35
✳

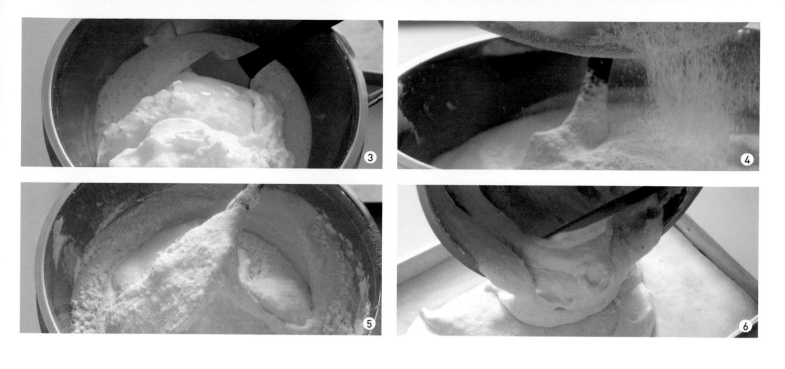

 400 g/14 oz plain flour

200 g/7 oz unsalted butter, cut into small pieces and chilled

100 g/3½ oz sugar

pinch of salt

2 eggs

Sweet Shortcrust Pastry

1. Place the flour, butter, sugar and salt on a work surface.

2. Using both hands, quickly rub the butter into the flour. If it is worked for too long, the butter will become warm and the dough will crumble later.

3. Separate one of the eggs. Add one egg and one egg yolk to the flour mixture and work in. Store the remaining egg white in the refrigerator for later use.

4. Knead the dough briskly and thoroughly until it is smooth and elastic.

Wrap in clingfilm and refrigerate for at least 1 hour.

Makes about 750 g /1 lb 10 oz.

■ Use this basic recipe to make delicious almond biscuits – simply substitute a quarter of the flour for finely chopped almonds. Prepare the dough as described, shape into biscuits and bake until golden brown.

* * * 75

Vanilla Sauce

Cut **1 vanilla pod** in half lengthways and scrape out the seeds with the back of a knife. Add the seeds and the pod to **250 ml/ 9 fl oz of milk** in a saucepan and bring to the boil. Meanwhile, separate **6 eggs.** Combine the egg yolks with **50 g/1¾ oz of sugar** and beat until fluffy. Bring some water to the boil in a long-handled saucepan, then leave to simmer. As soon as the milk boils, pour it through a sieve so that none of the residue from the vanilla pod is included in the sauce. Gradually add the hot milk to the egg-sugar mixture, stirring constantly. Heat the mixture over the simmering water and stir until it is thick enough to coat the back of a spoon. Place over a bowl of iced water and stir until cold.

■ **If the sauce becomes too hot, it will curdle. If this happens, pass it through a fine sieve. Stir in 1 tablespoon of cornflour and 2 tablespoons of milk and whisk them into the hot vanilla sauce. Return the sauce to the boil and it will be creamy once again.**

Chocolate Sauce

Slowly bring **125 ml/4 fl oz of milk, 100 ml/3½ fl oz of cream** and ½ **scraped vanilla pod** to the boil in a saucepan. Chop **100 g/3½ oz of plain chocolate** and **50 g/ 1¾ oz of milk chocolate** into small pieces and add to the milk mixture. Stir slowly with a whisk until the chocolate is melted. Remove from the heat, take out the vanilla pod and stir in **2 teaspoons of cognac, 20 g/⅔ oz of sugar** and **2½ tablespoons of vegetable oil.** Pour the sauce through a fine sieve and serve at room temperature.

■ **Use hazelnut oil in place of the vegetable oil for a nutty flavour.**

Caramel Sauce

Put **50 g/1¾ oz of sugar and 100 ml/ 3½ fl oz of water** into a small, long-handled saucepan and bring to the boil over a low heat. Simmer until the sugar is golden brown and evenly caramelized. Add **3½ tablespoons of water** to prevent the sugar browning further. Simmer for about 5 minutes until the water has evaporated. Add **250 ml/9 fl oz of milk**. Cut **1 vanilla pod** in half lengthways and scrape out the seeds with the back of a knife. Add the pod and the seeds to the milk and bring the mixture to the boil. Meanwhile, separate **6 eggs.** Combine the egg yolks with **30 g/1 oz of sugar** and beat until fluffy. Pour some water into a long-handled saucepan and bring to the boil, then leave to simmer. As soon as the milk boils, pour it through a sieve, so that no lumps are included in the sauce. Gradually add the hot milk to the egg-sugar mixture, stirring constantly. Heat the mixture over the simmering water and stir until it is thick enough to coat the back of a spoon. Place over a bowl of iced water and stir until cold.

Strawberry Sauce

Sprinkle **50 g/1¾ oz of icing sugar** over **250 g/9 oz of strawberries. Add 5 tablespoons of water** and purée with a hand-held blender to make a thin sauce. Pass the purée through a fine sieve and serve.

Apricot Sauce

Put **5 apricots** into boiling water for 10 seconds, then immediately plunge them into cold water to chill them. Peel and halve the apricots and remove the stones. Put the apricot halves, the juice of ½ **lemon, 50 g/1¾ oz of icing sugar** and **5 tablespoons of water** in a bowl and mix with a hand-held blender. Pass the mixture through a fine sieve and serve.

Kiwi Sauce

Peel **4 kiwi fruit,** put them in a bowl with **50 g/1¾ oz of icing sugar** and **5 tablespoons of water** and mix them with a hand-held blender. Pass the mixture through a fine sieve and serve.

■ **Kiwi fruit cannot be used with any dairy products, as they contain a curdling enzyme (just like pineapples do).**

800 g/1 lb 12 oz quark

200 ml/7 fl oz milk

100 ml/3½ fl oz single cream

5 eggs

1 lemon

50 g/1¾ oz unsalted butter

80 g/2¾ oz vanilla sugar

90 g/3¼ oz cornflour

pinch of salt

125 g/4½ oz sugar

250 g/9 oz Sweet Shortcrust Pastry
(see page 10)

German Cheesecake

1. Preheat the oven to 220°C /425°F/Gas Mark 7. Put the quark in a bowl, add the milk and cream and mix until smooth. Separate the eggs and put the egg whites in a covered bowl in the refrigerator. Rinse the lemon with hot water, then finely grate the zest. Cut the lemon in half and squeeze the juice into a bowl. Melt the butter in a small saucepan over a low heat.

2. Add the egg yolk, melted butter, half the vanilla sugar, the lemon juice, lemon zest and cornflour to the quark mixture, and stir with a wire whisk until smooth.

3. Beat the egg whites with the salt and sugar until holding soft peaks, then fold into the quark mixture.

4. Roll out the dough to a thickness of slightly less than 5 mm/¼ inch, and use to line a 23-cm/9-inch non-stick springform cake tin. Cut any excess crust from around the edges with a knife. Fill the crust with the quark mixture and smooth the surface. Bake in the preheated oven for about 5 minutes, then remove the cake from the oven. Insert a knife between the crust and the skin on top of the cake and make a cut all along the crust. Return to the oven and bake for a further 15 minutes. Remove the cake from the oven, leave to stand until it has sunk a little and reduce the oven temperature to 160°C/325°F/Gas Mark 3. Return the cake to the oven and bake for a further 35 minutes.

5. Remove from the oven, leave to cool, then take it out of the tin. Serve warm with the remaining vanilla sugar sprinkled on top.

■ German cheesecake tastes especially good slightly warm, but it's harder to cut that way – so be careful! Add 50 g/1¾ oz of rum-soaked raisins to the quark batter, if liked.

✳
✳ 120
✳

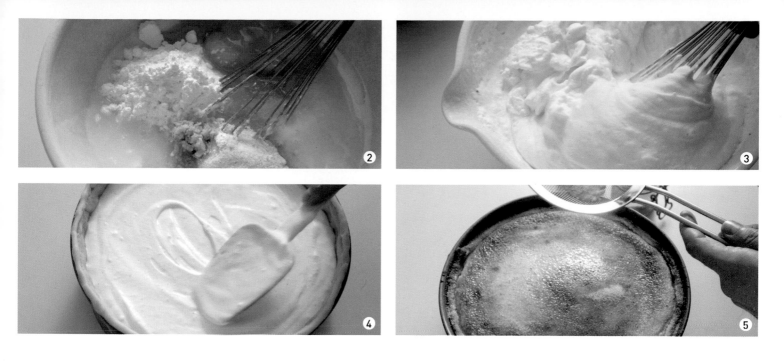

240 g/8½ oz plain flour

500 ml/18 fl oz milk

3 tbsp sugar

3 eggs

150 g/5½ oz butter

2 tbsp vegetable oil

Sweet Pancake Batter

1. Put the flour into a mixing bowl. Add half the milk and the sugar.

2. Whisk the batter until it is smooth and thick.

3. Pour in the remaining milk and beat in the eggs.

4. Melt the butter in a small saucepan until golden brown with a nutty odour.

5. Using the whisk, stir the butter into the batter a little at a time.

6. Heat the oil in a frying pan. Using a ladle, pour some pancake batter into the pan and spread it in a thin layer over the base by tilting the pan back and forth.

7. Using a spatula, loosen the batter from the edge of the pan and toss the pancake to turn. It takes some practice, but it really works! Otherwise, place a plate upside down over the pan and invert the pan so that the pancake falls onto the plate, then return the pancake to the pan to cook the other side.

8. Cook the pancake briefly after turning. Transfer the cooked pancakes to a plate and leave to cool before serving.

■ Serve the pancakes by spreading them with fresh jam, or rolling them up, sprinkling them with sugar and serving with lemon wedges for squeezing over. A fruit and cottage cheese filling with Vanilla Sauce (see page 12) is also delicious.

✳
✳ 25
✳

4 eggs

260 g/9¼ oz icing sugar

200 g/7 oz raspberries

200 g/7 oz wild strawberries

250 ml/9 fl oz double cream

seeds of 1 vanilla pod

①

Pavlova with Berries & Vanilla Cream

1. Preheat the oven to 120°C/250°F/ Gas Mark ½. Separate the eggs and chill the whites. Add the chilled egg whites to the bowl and beat with the whisk until holding soft peaks. Gradually add the sugar and beat until stiff.

2. Use a rubber spatula to put the beaten egg whites into a piping bag.

3. Pipe the egg white mixture into spirals on a baking tray covered with baking paper. Bake them in the preheated oven for approximately 35 minutes, then reduce the temperature to 110°C/225°F/ Gas Mark ¼ and leave the meringues to dry for 4 hours.

4. Hull the berries and put them into a bowl.

5. Cut the top off the baked meringues with a sharp, serrated knife. Whip the cream with the vanilla seeds and spread the mixture on the lower half of the meringues. Top with berries, set the lids over the berries at an angle and serve immediately.

+4 hours drying

✳
✳
✳

65

■ Try making a miniature version of these meringue cases. They won't take as long to dry and can be served with afternoon tea. They can also be prepared in advance and filled just before they are served. You can also use fruit sorbet as a filling instead of fresh fruit.

150 g/5½ oz plain chocolate

2 eggs

3 tbsp sugar

1 tbsp low-fat cocoa powder

1½ tbsp cognac

4 tbsp espresso

pinch of salt

200 ml/7 fl oz double cream, whipped

4 tbsp chocolate shavings, to decorate

Plain Chocolate Mousse

1. Put the chocolate in a heatproof bowl set over a saucepan of barely simmering water.

2. Separate the eggs and chill the egg whites in the refrigerator. Whisk the egg yolks with the sugar until foaming. Stir the cocoa, cognac and espresso into the egg mixture.

3. Add the warm melted chocolate.

4. Stir until combined.

5. Beat the egg whites with a pinch of salt until holding stiff peaks, then fold them into the chocolate mixture with a wire whisk. Fold in the whipped cream, and leave the mousse to chill in the refrigerator for at least 2 hours.

To serve, scoop out portions with a spoon and decorate with chocolate shavings.

✳
✳ **160**
✳

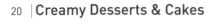

■ Put a ripe banana into a saucepan with 2 pieces of finely chopped stem ginger, the juice of ½ an orange and ½ a vanilla pod and bring to the boil. Add the mixture as an intermediate layer in the chocolate mousse and leave to chill in the refrigerator. Chocolate and bananas are an excellent combination and will turn the mousse into a wonderful dessert.

1 sachet powdered gelatine

700 ml/1¼ pints milk

100 g/3½ oz white chocolate

3 tbsp maple syrup

White Chocolate Mousse with Maple Syrup

1. Put the gelatine into a glass with 4 tablespoons of cold water. Stir and leave to soak for 10 minutes.

2. Heat the milk in a saucepan, then set aside 2 tablespoons. Break the chocolate into pieces, add to the pan and heat until dissolved.

3. Mix the gelatine with the reserved hot milk, then add to the chocolate-milk mixture and stir until completely dissolved.

4. Pour the chocolate mousse into a siphon with the aid of a funnel.

5. Add the maple syrup, close the siphon when it contains 750 ml/1⅓ pints of the mixture and shake well. Leave to cool in the refrigerator for about 1 hour.

To serve, insert two cartridges and pipe the fluffy mousse into small bowls.

■ The mousse can be prepared in advance using this method. At the last minute, you can serve it fresh in glasses and it will be particularly frothy and taste very fruity. Plain chocolate, nougat or even fruit purées can be added to the milk. However, fruit purées should not be cooked further and the quantity of gelatine must be increased by half because of the acid in the fruit.

* *
* **90**

4 eggs

80 g/2¾ oz sugar

seeds from ½ vanilla pod

2 tbsp cognac

1 tbsp Grand Marnier

500 g/1 lb 2 oz mascarpone cheese

150 g/5½ oz sponge fingers

200 ml/7 fl oz espresso

30 g/1 oz cocoa powder

Tiramisù

1. Separate the eggs and store the egg whites in the refrigerator for later use. Beat the yolks with the sugar and the vanilla seeds until fluffy.

2. Add the cognac and Grand Marnier and stir.

3. Using a rubber spatula, add the mascarpone cheese and whisk it into the mixture.

4. Dip the sponge fingers in the espresso for a maximum of 3 seconds, so that they are not completely saturated.

5. Put the ingredients in a bowl in alternating layers. Start with a layer of sponge fingers, then add a layer of the mascarpone cream and repeat the process. Top with cream and leave to chill in the refrigerator for at least 1 hour.

Remove from the refrigerator, sprinkle with the cocoa powder and serve immediately.

+1 hour cooling

✳✳✳ 40

■ If the cream becomes lumpy, add some hot milk and beat it in until the mixture is smooth.

 1 freshly made Sponge Cake (see page 8)

1 tbsp sugar

200 g/7 oz strawberries

200 g/7 oz strawberry jam

Strawberry Swiss Roll

1. Turn out the warm sponge cake onto a sheet of baking paper sprinkled with sugar. Carefully pull off the top layer of baking paper.

2. Roll up the sponge cake and leave to cool. Meanwhile, hull and thinly slice the strawberries.

3. Unroll the sponge cake and spread the strawberry jam over it. Distribute the sliced strawberries over the jam.

4. Roll up the filled sponge cake using both hands, applying a light pressure to keep any hollow spaces out of the roll. Leave to cool for 15 minutes, then cut it into slices about 2.5 cm/1 inch thick.

Arrange on a platter and serve.

✳
✳
✳
60

■ Rubbing the top sheet of baking paper with moist kitchen paper will make it easier to pull it off the top of the sponge cake after it is turned out of the tray.

250 ml/9 fl oz milk

80 g/2¾ oz caster sugar

3 eggs, separated

20 g/⅔ oz cornflour

30 g/1 oz butter

1 vanilla pod

250 g/9 oz ready-made puff pastry

200 g/7 oz mixed berries

3 tbsp water

30 g/1 oz granulated sugar

3 tbsp white wine

1½ sheets leaf gelatine

icing sugar, for dusting

zest of 1 orange, to decorate

Little Fruit Tarts

1. Preheat the oven to 180°C/350°F/ Gas Mark 4. Mix 4 tablespoons of the milk with the caster sugar, 1 egg yolk and the cornflour. Cut the butter into small pieces and chill in the refrigerator. Cut the vanilla pod in half lengthways and scrape out the seeds with the back of a knife. Put the remaining milk into a saucepan with the vanilla seeds and pod and bring to the boil. Pour through a sieve into a clean saucepan and return to the heat. Pour the prepared mixture of milk, egg yolk, sugar and cornflour slowly into the hot milk and leave to thicken.

2. Stir the custard and the chilled butter over a bowl of iced water, cover and leave to cool.

3. Cut the pastry into triangles and tubes and assemble as shown in the photograph. Lightly beat the remaining egg yolks with a fork and use to brush the pastry. Prick the tart bases with a fork.

4. Bake in the preheated oven for 12–15 minutes, then leave to cool. Fill with the vanilla cream to just below the rim.

5. Top the vanilla cream with berries. Put the water, sugar and wine into a small saucepan and bring to the boil. Meanwhile, put the gelatine sheets into a bowl of cold water and leave to soak for 10 minutes. Add to the pan, dissolve and leave to cool. Coat the berries with the glaze.

Dust the tarts with icing sugar, decorate with a twist of orange zest and serve.

■ The little tarts can be topped with any kind of berries you like. A large slice of puff pastry with vanilla cream and fresh strawberries is also a delicious alternative to a cake.

✳
✳
✳
75

 ½ vanilla pod

500 ml/18 fl oz cream

100 g/3½ oz sugar

1 tbsp coffee beans

3 sheets leaf gelatine

Panna Cotta with Coffee

1. Cut the vanilla pod in half lengthways. Scrape out the seeds with the back of a knife and add them to the cream. Put the cream into a saucepan with the scraped vanilla pod, sugar and coffee beans and bring to the boil. Meanwhile, soak the gelatine sheets in cold water for about 10 minutes, until soft.

2. Remove the boiled cream mixture from the heat. Drain the gelatine, add to the hot cream and leave to dissolve.

3. Pour the cream through a sieve into a measuring jug.

4. Pour into glasses and leave to chill in the refrigerator for at least 3 hours until set.

Remove from the refrigerator, put the glasses into hot water for a moment, then turn out the panna cotta and serve.

* * * 210

■ Sprinkle the panna cotta with crushed almond biscuits or amaretti and decorate it with amarena cherries. For a lighter panna cotta, substitute half of the cream for milk.

3 eggs

250 g/9 oz sugar

1 tbsp vanilla sugar

100 ml/3½ fl oz milk

100 g/3½ oz unsalted butter, plus extra for greasing

250 g/9 oz plain flour, plus extra for dusting

2 tsp baking powder

pinch of salt

1 tsp cornflour

200 g/7 oz redcurrants

200 g/7 oz blueberries

Redcurrant & Blueberry Meringue Cake

1. Preheat the oven to 180°C/350°F/ Gas Mark 4. Separate the eggs and put the whites in the refrigerator. Put the egg yolks into a mixing bowl with 150 g/5½ oz of the sugar and the vanilla sugar and beat well. Put the milk and butter into a saucepan and bring to the boil, then add to the sugar-egg mixture and stir well.

2. Sift the flour and the baking powder into the bowl and mix.

3. Grease a 28-cm/11-inch springform tin with butter and dust with flour. Pour in the cake batter and bake in the preheated oven for 18 minutes. Remove from the oven and leave to cool slightly. Increase the oven temperature to 220°C/425°F/ Gas Mark 7.

4. Using an electric mixer, beat the egg whites, salt and the remaining sugar until creamy. Add the cornflour and beat on the highest setting for 1 minute, until holding stiff peaks. Carefully mix the fruit into the egg whites, reserving 1 tablespoon of each type of berry.

5. Spread the meringue over the baked cake.

6. Sprinkle the reserved berries over the meringue. Return the cake to the oven and bake for about 15 minutes. Remove from the oven and leave to cool.

Transfer to a platter to serve.

■ After the cake has cooled, spread 3-cm/1¼-inch thick layers of vanilla and chocolate ice cream over it. Cover with the meringue and bake for 5 minutes at 240°C/ 475°F/Gas Mark 9. Remove from the oven and serve immediately. This makes an especially delicious and festive dessert.

***100

5 eggs

80 g/2¾ oz sponge fingers

3 tbsp Grand Marnier

50 g/1¾ oz butter

1 vanilla pod

30 g/1 oz cornflour

200 ml/7 fl oz milk

100 g/3½ oz caster sugar

pinch of salt

Vanilla Sponge Soufflés

1. Separate the eggs and put 1 egg white in the refrigerator for later use. Cut the sponge fingers into 5-mm/¼-inch cubes, place in a dish and pour over the Grand Marnier. Allow 30 g/1 oz of the butter to soften at room temperature. Cut the vanilla pod in half lengthways and scrape out the seeds with the back of a knife. Beat the 4 remaining egg whites until holding stiff peaks, cover and leave to chill in the refrigerator. Mix the cornflour with 2½ tablespoons of the milk. Put the remaining milk in a saucepan, add the remaining butter, 70 g/2½ oz of the sugar, the vanilla seeds, vanilla pod and salt, and bring to the boil.

2. Use a brush to coat four ramekins with the softened butter. Line the ramekins by putting some sugar into each of the ramekins and tilting them, as shown in the photograph, so that some sugar coats the sides and the surplus falls into the bowl.

3. Add the cold milk and the cornflour to the boiling milk mixture, stirring constantly with a wire whisk for 2 minutes. The cornflour will thicken the milk. Cover with clingfilm and leave to cool. Preheat a fan oven to 180°C/350°F/Gas Mark 4. Line a baking tin with baking paper, pour in water to a depth of 2 fingers to make a bain-marie, and put it in the preheated oven until the water starts to boil.

*
**
***
90

■ Cover the soufflé mixture with clingfilm while cooling to prevent a skin forming.

Have your guests seated before serving – guests wait for a soufflé but soufflés don't wait for guests.

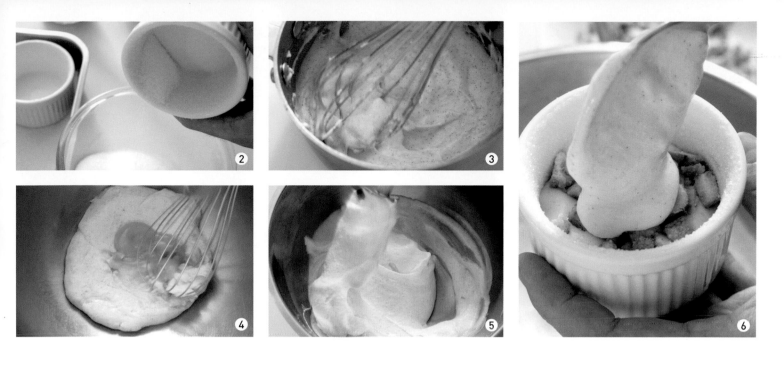

4. Stir the egg yolks into the cooled mixture. It must be cool to prevent the egg curdling. Pass the mixture through a sieve to remove any lumps.

5. Fold the beaten egg whites carefully into the egg yolk mixture with a rubber spatula. Stir gently, so that none of the trapped air escapes. Divide the sponge finger cubes between the ramekins.

6. Spoon the soufflé mixture on top of the sponge finger cubes. Place the ramekins in the bain-marie and bake the soufflés in the preheated oven for 20 minutes. They are cooked when they turn golden yellow and reach a height of 2–3 cm/¾–1¼ inches above the rims of the ramekins.

Remove the soufflés from the oven, turn out onto individual plates and serve immediately with Chocolate Sauce (see page 12).

30 g/1 oz butter, softened, plus extra for greasing

20 g/⅔ oz flour

1 vanilla pod

80 g/2¾ oz walnuts

20 g/⅔ oz plain chocolate

3 eggs

80 g/2¾ oz caster sugar

200 ml/7 fl oz milk

icing sugar, for dusting

①

Walnut Soufflés

1. Mix the butter with the flour in a small bowl to make a beurre manié for use as a thickener. Cut the vanilla pod in half lengthways and scrape out the seeds with the back of a knife. Roughly chop the walnuts and chocolate. Separate the eggs. Beat the egg whites until holding soft peaks, then cover and chill in the refrigerator. Grease four ramekins and 'line' the rims with caster sugar (see page 34).

2. Put the milk, walnuts, vanilla seeds and vanilla pod into a saucepan and bring to the boil. Remove the vanilla pod and stir in the beurre manié.

3. Simmer for 3 minutes, stirring constantly, until the mixture thickens. Cover with clingfilm and leave to cool. Meanwhile, preheat the oven to 200°C/400°F/Gas Mark 6. Pour water into a baking tin to a depth of two fingers to make a bain-marie. When the mixture has cooled to room temperature, stir in the egg yolks. Gently fold in the beaten egg whites with a rubber spatula. Fill the ramekins two-thirds full with the mixture and bake them in the bain-marie for 20 minutes, or until the soufflés have risen 2 cm/¾ inch above the ramekin rims.

Sprinkle with the icing sugar and serve immediately.

■ You can use this basic recipe to whip up different kinds of soufflé in no time. Just substitute other ingredients for the walnuts. For best results, use hazelnuts, chestnut purée, roasted almonds or desiccated coconut. However, if you are using coconut, white chocolate should be substituted for the plain chocolate.

 6 eggs

100 g/3½ oz caster sugar

200 ml/7 fl oz sparkling white wine

4 tbsp Marsala

juice of ½ lemon

1. Hot Zabaglione

1. Separate the eggs. Put the egg yolks, sugar, wine, Marsala and lemon juice into a bowl.

2. Beat the mixture over a saucepan of barely simmering water, scraping the edges of the bowl to avoid lumps being created.

3. The mixture will become lighter in colour and more viscous, and will increase in volume.

4. The zabaglione is ready when it has a creamy, glossy consistency.

Pour into glasses and serve immediately.

*** 30

2. Pistachio Zabaglione

Separate **4 eggs**. Beat the egg yolks with **60 g/2¼ oz of sugar** and **100 ml/3½ fl oz of sparkling white wine** in a bain-marie as in the basic zabaglione recipe. Put **1 sheet of leaf gelatine** into warm water, dissolve it, then add it to the zabaglione. Stir this mixture over a bowl of iced water until it is cold. Grind **60 g/2¼ oz of pistachio nuts** in a blender until they are almost like a paste and add them to the zabaglione. Whip **100 ml/3½ fl oz of double cream** until holding soft peaks and fold it into the mixture.

Pour the zabaglione into glasses and serve with crushed pistachios sprinkled on top.

3. Campari Zabaglione

Separate **4 eggs**. Beat the egg yolks with **60 g/2½ oz of sugar** and **80 ml/2¾ fl oz of Campari** in a bain-marie as in the basic zabaglione recipe. Finely grate some **orange zest** and add to the zabaglione. Heat **1 sheet of leaf gelatine** in the juice of **1 orange** until dissolved, then add it to the zabaglione. Stir this mixture over a bowl of iced water until cold. Whip **150 ml/5 fl oz of double cream** until holding soft peaks and fold it in.

Pour the zabaglione into glasses and serve topped with strips of orange zest.

 150 g/5½ oz caster sugar

125 ml/4 fl oz water

3 eggs

seeds from 1 vanilla pod

2 tsp amaretto

500 ml/18 fl oz double cream

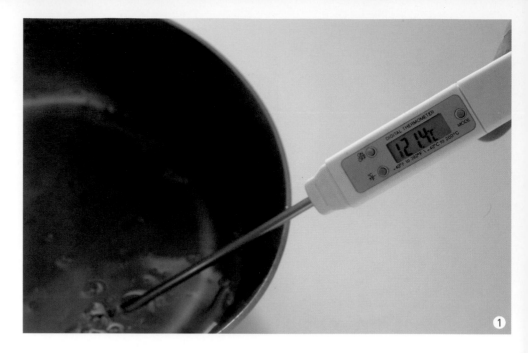

Vanilla Ice Cream Parfait

1. Put the sugar and water in a saucepan and heat to precisely 121°C/250°F. Use a sugar thermometer.

2. Separate the eggs and put the egg yolks into a metal bowl. Gradually mix the sugar syrup with the egg yolks, stirring constantly with a wire whisk so that the egg doesn't solidify.

3. Mix in the vanilla seeds and the amaretto, then whisk the mixture until creamy. Stir it over a bowl of iced water until cold.

4. Beat the cream until holding stiff peaks, then stir in one third of the cream with a wire whisk. Carefully fold in the remaining cream.

5. Put the mixture into a mould and put it in the freezer for at least 6 hours. Hold the mould briefly under hot running hot water to turn out the parfait. Use a hot knife to cut 1-cm/½-inch thick slices and serve immediately. Wrap any remaining parfait in clingfilm and store in the freezer.

Variations on the parfait can be made by adding any of the following ingredients:
- 200 g/7 oz of strawberry purée
- 150 g/5½ oz of passion fruit purée with 3 tablespoons of coconut liqueur
- 50 g/1¾ oz of roasted almonds, 120 g/4½ oz of coarsely chopped amarena cherries and 2 teaspoons of cherry liqueur
- 200 g/7 oz of apricot purée with 2 teaspoons of amaretto

+6 hours freezing

* \
* * 40
* \

■ You can also surprise your guests with an ice cream soufflé by making a collar from baking paper, putting it into a miniature soufflé dish and pouring in some parfait mixture. The parfait creates the effect of a soufflé, but it is made with ice cream.

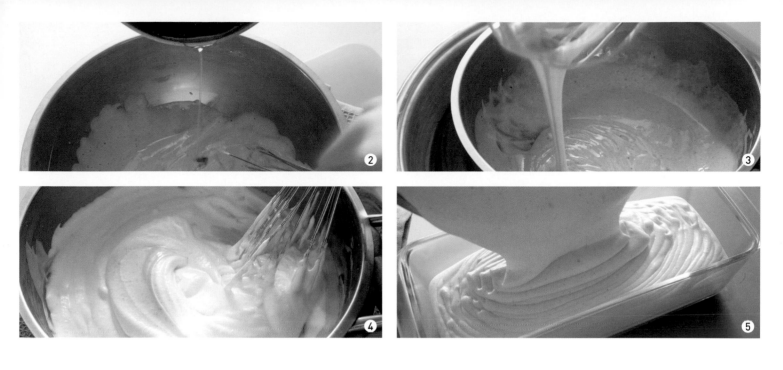

 5 eggs

125 g/4½ oz caster sugar

500 ml/18 fl oz milk

1 vanilla pod

8 sheets leaf gelatine

400 ml/14 fl oz double cream, whipped

Bavarian Cream

1. Separate the eggs and whisk the egg yolks with the sugar until the mixture is almost white. Prepare a bain-marie, taking care that the bowl does not touch the water.

2. Put the milk, vanilla pod and vanilla seeds into a separate saucepan, bring to the boil and, using a wire whisk, stir gradually into the egg-sugar mixture.

3. Slowly heat the mixture in the bain-marie over a low heat, stirring constantly with a wooden spoon so that the egg doesn't solidify at the edge of the bowl.

4. Stir the mixture until the egg thickens. The mixture is ready when it coats the back of the wooden spoon.

5. Soften the gelatine sheets in warm water, squeeze them and then mix them with the whipped cream. Stir over a bowl of iced water until cold.

6. Carefully fold some of the whipped cream into the egg, sugar and milk mixture and gently mix with a whisk.

■ You can also make a coffee cream by adding some espresso to the egg mixture before folding in the cream. Increase the quantity of gelatine sheets to 9.

7. Fold in the remaining cream, turning the whisk with your wrist, as if you were using a stirring spoon. Pour into dishes, cover and chill in the refrigerator.

Serve the cream with a fruit sauce (see page 13) or fresh fruit.

8 eggs

 200 g/7 oz caster sugar

¼ tsp ground cinnamon, plus extra for dusting

800 ml/1⅓ pints red wine

Wine Chaudeau

1. Separate the eggs and put the egg yolks into a stainless steel bowl. Add the sugar and the cinnamon.

2. Pour in the wine and mix it in with a wire whisk. Put 2 cm/¾ inches of water into a long-handled saucepan and bring to the boil over a high heat.

3. Place the bowl over the saucepan.

4. Beat the mixture vigorously until the volume increases threefold and the custard is thick and creamy.

Remove from the heat and pour into glasses. Serve hot, with some cinnamon sprinkled on top.

■ Hot red wine chaudeau is especially delicious when served with baked pears, peaches or apples. If you substitute Prosecco or Marsala for the red wine, you will produce a mouthwatering zabaglione.

✳ ✳ ✳ 30

4 eggs

100 g/3½ oz caster sugar, plus extra to taste

pinch of ground cinnamon

400 ml/14 fl oz red wine

2 sheets leaf gelatine

300 ml/10 fl oz double cream, whipped

8 sponge fingers

Cold Wine Cream

1. Make a Wine Chaudeau from the egg yolks, sugar, cinnamon and half the wine (see page 44). Put the gelatine sheets into a bowl of cold water and leave to stand for about 10 minutes, then squeeze them and transfer to the wine chaudeau to dissolve. Pour the mixture into a bowl and leave to cool.

2. Meanwhile, put the remaining wine into a saucepan, bring to the boil and cook until it has reduced to a volume of 4 tablespoons.

3. Add the whipped cream and almost the entire wine reduction to the cold wine chaudeau, reserving a little for decoration.

4. Carefully fold the cream and the reduction into the cold wine chaudeau. The red wine reduction will give its colour to the wine chaudeau and will intensify its flavour.

Break the sponge fingers into pieces and put them into glasses. Add the cream on top and leave to cool for 1 hour. Mix some red wine reduction with sugar to taste, drizzle it over the wine cream and serve.

+1 hour cooling

■ White wine can also be used for this cold wine cream. If you make a white wine cream, use white wine to make the wine reduction as well. Small deseeded green grapes can also be added to the sponge fingers. Red grapes go better with the red wine cream. It tastes a little fresher if they are added!

650 ml/1 pint coconut milk

125 g/4½ oz coarsely ground tapioca

60 g/2¼ oz demerara sugar

1 vanilla pod

pinch of salt

100 ml/3½ fl oz orange juice

3 star anise

1 tbsp granulated sugar

10 g/¼ oz cornflour

1½ tbsp orange liqueur

2 oranges

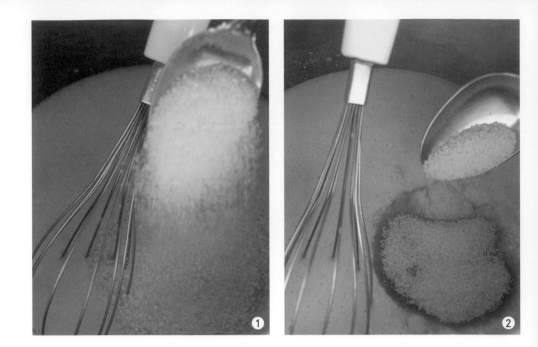

Tapioca-coconut Pudding

1. Put the coconut milk into a saucepan and bring to the boil. Slowly sprinkle in the tapioca and stir with a wire whisk.

2. Add the demerara sugar and simmer for 5 minutes. Scrape out the vanilla pod and add the vanilla seeds and the salt.

3. The pudding is cooked once it has a firm, even consistency. Pour it into glasses or bowls, cover with clingfilm and leave to cool.

4. Put the orange juice, star anise and granulated sugar into a small saucepan and bring to the boil.

5. Mix the cornflour with the orange liqueur and add to the orange juice mixture to thicken.

6. Peel and segment the oranges and add the slices to the thickened sauce. Remove the sauce from the heat and leave to cool.

Pour the sauce over the tapioca pudding and serve.

■ The coconut milk must not be thickened. If the pudding sticks to the base of the pan, stop stirring and pour it out immediately. Green tea ice cream or stewed papaya are perfect accompaniments to this pudding.

8 sponge fingers

300 g/10½ oz cherries, plus extra to serve

2 tbsp granulated sugar

½ tsp ground cinnamon

1½ tbsp cherry liqueur

1 packet spring roll wrappers (12 × 12 cm/4½ × 4½ inches)

1 egg white, for brushing

2 litres/3½ pints vegetable oil, for deep-frying

icing sugar, for dusting

Spring Rolls with Cherry Filling

1. Put the sponge fingers into a bowl and crush.

2. Halve and stone the cherries and add to the sponge fingers.

3. Add the sugar and the cinnamon.

4. Drizzle with the cherry liqueur and mix well.

5. Lay the spring roll wrappers on the work surface. Put 2 tablespoons of the cherry filling in the centre of each. Brush the edges with egg white.

6. Fold two opposite corners into the centre and brush the edges with egg white.

7. Fold in the third corner and brush the lower section with egg white.

8. Fold the lower section onto the filling and press down lightly. Brush the upper section with egg white and roll up the wrap completely.

9. Put the oil in a large saucepan and heat to 160°C/325°F. Add the spring rolls and deep-fry for about 5 minutes, or until they are golden.

10. Remove the spring rolls and drain on kitchen paper.

Arrange the spring rolls on plates, sprinkle with icing sugar and serve with whole cherries.

■ These spring rolls can also be filled with other fruit such as plums, morello cherries, mangoes, bananas or grapes. Filling with vanilla cream is also an option, although you will need to use some soaked broken sponge fingers to give the filling structure.

*\
*\
* **45**

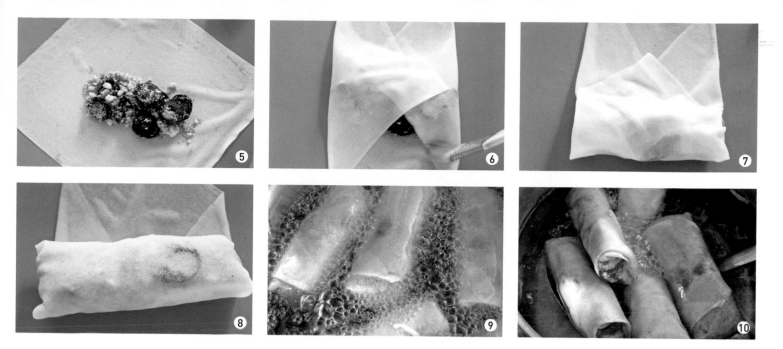

125 g/4½ oz butter, softened

60 g/2¼ oz soft light brown sugar

3 eggs

50 g/1¾ oz flaked almonds

100 g/3½ oz white breadcrumbs

4 peaches

8 fresh lavender sprigs, plus extra to decorate

1 vanilla pod

4 tsp honey

3 tbsp peach liqueur

Baked Peaches with Lavender

1. Preheat the oven to 220°C/425°F/ Gas Mark 7. Put the butter and the sugar into a mixing bowl and beat until fluffy. Separate the eggs and gradually beat the yolks into the mixture.

2. Toast the flaked almonds in a frying pan until golden, then leave to cool. Add the almonds and the breadcrumbs to the butter-egg mixture and mix well.

3. Score the peach skins lightly with a knife, then put the fruit into a heatproof bowl, pour over boiling water and leave to stand for about 10–15 seconds. Remove the peaches with a slotted spoon and place them in iced water to cool.

4. Remove the skins and cut the peaches in half. Lay the lavender sprigs in the base of a baking dish. Remove the peach stones and put the peach halves, cut side up, on top of the lavender sprigs.

5. Fill the peaches with the almond mixture. Cut the vanilla pod in half lengthways and divide it into 3-cm/ 1¼-inch lengths. Drizzle the peaches with the honey and the peach liqueur and bake in the preheated oven for about 20 minutes.

Arrange the peaches on plates, decorate with the vanilla strips and lavender sprigs and serve.

■ Baked apples with raisin filling: 40 g/1½ oz of fluffy whipped butter, 60 g/2¼ oz of lightly toasted chopped almonds, 40 g/1½ oz of raisins (softened in 2 tablespoons of tea), 50 g/1¾ oz of crustless white bread cubes, 50 g/1¾ oz of marzipan, 8 small red apples with stems, 1 tablespoon of sugar, 1 tablespoon of honey, 5 cloves and 2 cinnamon sticks. Prepare these ingredients in the same way as in the baked peaches recipe and cook for the same length of time.

 500 g/1 lb 2 oz strawberries

10 fresh mint leaves

½ tsp green peppercorns

3 tbsp icing sugar

600 ml/1 pint water

1 litre/1¾ pints vegetable oil

250 g/9 oz fine noodles

Fried Fine Noodles in Strawberry Gazpacho

1. Hull and halve the strawberries, reserving two to decorate, and put them into a bowl. Add the mint leaves and the peppercorns.

2. Add 2 tablespoons of the sugar.

3. Pour in the water and mix, then transfer to a food processor and purée. Pour the purée into a bowl and leave to cool in the refrigerator for about 1 hour.

4. Heat the oil to 160°C/325°F in a small saucepan. Using scissors, cut the noodles in four, add to the pan in batches and fry for a few seconds.

5. Drain the fried noodles on kitchen paper and sprinkle them with the remaining sugar while still warm.

Pour the gazpacho into chilled bowls and top with the noodles. Halve the reserved strawberries and place 1 half in each bowl. Serve immediately, before the noodles absorb the liquid.

120

■ Watermelon, flavoured with a little vodka, can be used instead of strawberries.

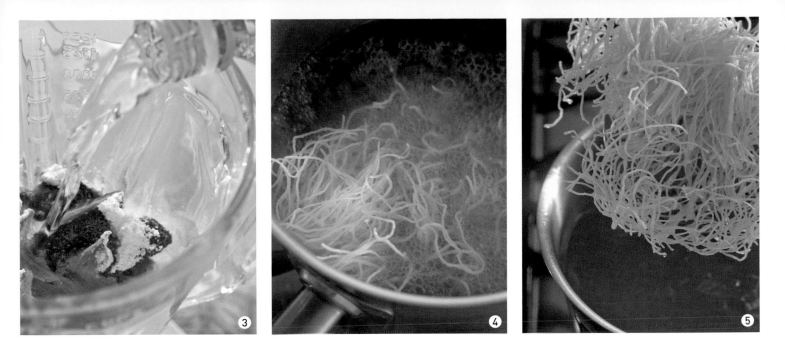

1 tbsp lemon juice

125 ml/4 fl oz low-fat Greek-style yogurt

125 ml/4 fl oz crème fraîche

90 g/3¼ oz icing sugar

150 g/5½ oz strawberry purée

4 sheets leaf gelatine

125 ml/4 fl oz double cream

2 eggs

30 g/1 oz granulated sugar

3 strawberries, hulled and sliced, to decorate

Strawberry Yogurt Mousse

1. Combine the lemon juice with the yogurt, crème fraîche, icing sugar and two thirds of the strawberry purée. Place the gelatine sheets in a bowl of cold water and leave to soak for 10 minutes, then squeeze out the moisture, transfer to a small saucepan and leave to dissolve. Mix the gelatine with the yogurt mixture.

2. Whip the cream until holding stiff peaks and then fold carefully into the mixture with a wire whisk.

3. Separate the eggs. Put the egg whites into a bowl, add the granulated sugar and beat until holding stiff peaks. Slowly fold them into the mixture.

Pour the mixture into glasses and chill in the refrigerator for 1 hour. Add a little of the remaining strawberry purée to each glass, decorate with the strawberry slices and serve.

120

250 g/9 oz bananas, plus extra to decorate

juice of 2 lemons

4 tbsp banana liqueur

30 g/1 oz butter

2½ sheets leaf gelatine

125 ml/4 fl oz double cream

2 eggs

60 g/2¼ oz sugar

2 tsp vanilla sugar

4 tbsp Chocolate Sauce (see page 12), to serve

Banana Mousse

1. Thinly slice the bananas, then drizzle with lemon juice to prevent discoloration. Put the bananas, banana liqueur and butter into a saucepan and bring to the boil. Purée with a hand-held blender and strain through a sieve. Place the gelatine sheets in a bowl of cold water and leave to soak for 10 minutes, then squeeze out the moisture, transfer to a small saucepan and leave to dissolve. Stir into the banana purée and leave to cool.

2. Whip the cream until holding soft peaks, then fold carefully into the chilled banana purée.

3. Separate the eggs. Put the egg whites into a bowl and beat until they are light and fluffy, then carefully add the sugar and vanilla sugar. Beat until holding stiff peaks, then fold into the mousse, and pour into individual glasses. Chill in the refrigerator for at least 2 hours.

Decorate with some unpeeled banana slices and drizzle chocolate sauce on top.

■ You will need approximately 3 bananas to yield 250 g/9 oz peeled bananas. You must weigh the bananas precisely for the mousse to be a success.

160 ✳
✳
✳

250 g/9 oz unsalted butter

450 g/1 lb sugar

50 g/1¾ oz vanilla sugar

4 eggs

180 g/6¼ oz cocoa powder

250 g/9 oz plain flour, sifted

1 tsp baking powder

pinch of salt

150 g/5½ oz ground almonds

Chocolate Brownies

1. Preheat the oven to 180°C/350°F/Gas Mark 4. Slowly melt the butter in a wide saucepan. Add the sugar and vanilla sugar and mix. Remove from the heat and stir in the eggs one at a time.

2. Add the cocoa powder and stir with a whisk, then add the flour, baking powder, salt and ground almonds, mixing evenly.

3. Spread the mixture over the base of a non-stick baking tray and smooth the surface. Bake in the preheated oven for about 35 minutes. Remove from the oven and leave to cool. Turn out of the tray and cut into 4-cm/1½-inch squares.

Serve warm, with a scoop of vanilla ice cream, if liked.

■ **For a more intense chocolate flavour, chop some plain chocolate and stir it into the brownie batter.**

* **60** *
*

100 g/3½ oz soft light brown sugar

250 g/9 oz unsalted butter

400 g/14 oz granulated sugar

30 g/1 oz vanilla sugar

280 g/10 oz walnuts

4 eggs, beaten

180 g/6¼ oz cocoa powder

220 g/7¾ oz plain flour

1 tsp baking powder

pinch of salt

Walnut Caramel Brownies

1. Preheat the oven to 180°C/350°F/Gas Mark 4. Put the brown sugar into a wide saucepan over a medium heat and heat until caramelized. Add 100 ml/3½ fl oz cold water and dissolve the caramelized sugar. Add the butter and heat until melted, then remove the pan from the heat. Add the granulated sugar and vanilla sugar and mix. Roughly chop 200 g/7 oz of the walnuts and set aside.

2. Gradually stir in the eggs, then add the cocoa powder. Sift together the flour, baking powder and salt into the mixture. Add the chopped walnuts and mix.

3. Spread the mixture over the base of a non-stick baking tray and smooth the surface. Add the remaining walnuts. Bake in the preheated oven for about 35 minutes. Remove from the oven and leave to cool.

Turn out of the tray and cut into 4-cm/1½-inch squares. Serve warm, with a scoop of vanilla ice cream, if liked.

■ Brownies also taste good with a variety of other nuts, such as macadamia nuts, pecan nuts or Brazil nuts.

60 ✳ ✳ ✳

500 g/1 lb 2 oz Sweet Shortcrust Pastry (see page 10)

flour, for dusting

100 g/3½ oz fruit jam, such as raspberry, redcurrant or apricot

1 tbsp icing sugar, to decorate

1

Jam-filled Biscuits

1. Preheat the oven to 200°C/400°F/ Gas Mark 6. Roll out the dough on a lightly floured work surface to a thickness of slightly less than 2 mm/⅛ inch. Flip the dough constantly as you roll, sprinkling more flour each time so that it doesn't stick to the work surface.

2. Cut out shapes from the dough with biscuit cutters.

3. Lay a piece of baking paper in a baking tray, then arrange the shapes on the tray. Bake in the preheated oven for 8–10 minutes. They will cook quickly, so do take care not to allow them to burn.

4. Remove the biscuits from the baking tray and leave to cool. Spread jam on half the biscuits.

5. Place the remaining biscuits on top to make a sandwich.

Sprinkle with icing sugar and arrange on a plate to serve.

* * * 50

■ If you don't have any biscuit cutters, use the rim of a glass.

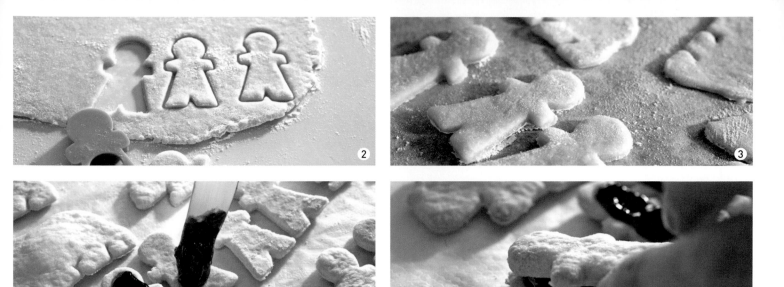

- 100 g/3½ oz unsalted butter

- 100 g/3½ oz icing sugar

- 80 g/2¾ oz granulated sugar

- ½ tsp salt

- 150 g/5½ oz pecan nuts

- 175 g/6 oz plain flour

- 1 tsp baking powder

- 1 egg

- cornflour, for dusting

①

Butter Pecan Cookies

1. On a work surface, rub the butter into the icing sugar, granulated sugar and the salt with your hands, working quickly so the butter doesn't get too warm. Finely grind half the pecan nuts, then roughly chop the remainder.

2. Sift together the flour and baking powder into the butter mixture and work in. Mix the ground and chopped nuts into the dough.

3. Add the egg and knead, again working quickly so the butter doesn't get too soft and the dough doesn't become sticky.

4. Dust your hands with flour and roll the dough into a 5-cm/2-inch diameter roll. Cover with clingfilm and chill in the refrigerator for 1 hour.

5. Meanwhile, preheat the oven to 180°C /350°F/Gas Mark 4. Lay a piece of baking paper on the base of a baking tray. Cut the dough into 2-cm/¾-inch thick slices and spread them out on the tray, leaving a little space between them to allow for spreading. Bake in the preheated oven for about 20 minutes, until golden. Remove from the oven and leave to cool. They can be stored for several days in an airtight container.

Serve with cold milk, fresh coffee or hot chocolate.

■ For chocolate biscuits, work 200 g/7 oz of chopped plain or white chocolate into the dough with the nuts, then bake as directed.

INDEX